P9-BXZ-152

Who Pooped in the Park?

Written by Gary D. Robson

Illustrated by Robert Rath

FARCOUNTRY
PRESS

To my brother, Keith.
- Gary

For Lucy and Thomas, my poop experts.
- Robert

ISBN 13: 978-1-56037-327-8
ISBN 10: 1-56037-327-X

© 2006 Farcountry Press
Text © 2006 Gary D. Robson
Illustrations © 2006 Farcountry Press

This book may not be reproduced in whole or in part by any means (with the exception of short quotes for the purpose of review) without the permission of the publisher.

For more information on our books,
write Farcountry Press, P.O. Box 5630, Helena, MT 59604;
call (800) 821-3874; or visit www.farcountrypress.com.

Book design by Robert Rath.
Created, produced, and designed in the United States.
Printed in China.

11 10 09 08 07 06   1 2 3 4 5 6

Library of Congress Cataloging-in-Publication Data

Robson, Gary D.
   Who pooped in the park?. Sequoia and Kings Canyon National Parks / [Gary D. Robson, Robert Rath].
     p. cm.
   ISBN-13: 978-1-56037-327-8
   1. Animal tracks--California--Sequoia National Park--Juvenile literature. 2. Animal tracks--
California--Kings Canyon National Park--Juvenile literature. I. Rath, Robert. II. Title.
   QL768.R64 2006
   591.9794'86--dc22

                    2005014576

"Dad? I have to go to the bathroom."
Michael squirmed in the back seat.

"We'll be at our campground in just
half an hour," said Dad. "We're in
Kings Canyon National Park now."

3

"He's just nervous," said Michael's sister. "He thinks a bear's gonna eat him." She growled at Michael and made her fingers look like claws.

"Stop it, Emily," said Mom. "Nobody is getting eaten by anything."

Michael was very excited about the trip,
but Emily was right. He *was* nervous.

He had just read a book about grizzly bears.
He knew how big they could get.

And he was afraid that a hungry bear would eat
just about anything—maybe even a boy.

5

"I *am* kind of scared of grizzly bears," admitted Michael.

"Don't worry," Dad told him. "There are no grizzlies in California anymore. Just black bears."

Mom held Michael's hand and said, "We'll show you how to count a black bear's toes and never get close enough to be scared."

"Here's our campsite. Let's set up the tent. Then we can go for a walk and we'll show you what we mean," Dad said.

Michael was pretty worried about bear toes, but tried not to show it.

"Let's hurry!" said Emily. "I want to see some animals!"

Once the tent was up, the whole family went for a hike.

Emily started to complain before they even left the campground. "I haven't seen any animals yet. Maybe there aren't any here!"

the STRAIGHT POOP

Ringtails are closely related to raccoons. While ringtails are sometimes called "ringtail cats," they are not related to either cats or the ringtail lemurs you sometimes see at the zoo.

"Sure there are," said Dad. "Let's see what we can learn about them from their *sign*."

"Sign?" said Michael. "You mean like a sign at the zoo?"

GREAT GRAY OWL

MULE DEER

BOBCAT

9

"By the word 'sign,' I mean a clue that an animal has left behind," Dad replied.

Mom said, "See all the bark stripped off of that tree? That's a sign of a porcupine having its lunch. Look around the base of the tree and I'll bet we'll find more sign."

the STRAIGHT POOP

Porcupines love to eat bark. Sometimes they'll climb a tree and eat the bark all the way around, killing the tree.

Michael was starting to get excited. "Look! I found tracks!"

"Right," said Mom. "Those are porcupine tracks. See the marks where it dragged its tail?"

the STRAIGHT POOP

Porcupines can't throw their quills, as some people believe. The quills are very sharp, so it's best to leave porcupines alone.

"And there's porcupine scat over here," said Dad.

"*Scat?*" asked Emily, looking a little less grumpy. "What's *scat?*"

"It's the word hikers and trackers use for animal poop," Dad replied.

"See, Michael," said Dad. "We don't have to get up close to an animal to learn about it. Instead of a close encounter of the *scary* kind, we'll have a close encounter of the *poopy* kind."

Everybody laughed, and Mom made a gross-out face.

"Dad! Mom! Look over here! I found bunny scat!" yelled Michael. "It's just like what we have in Fluffy's cage."

"We came all this way for *that*?" grumbled Emily. "Michael's bunny makes plenty of poop at home."

the STRAIGHT POOP

Rabbits eat their own scat! They do this to get as much nutrition from the food as they can. The little brown balls are scat that's already been through twice.

the STRAIGHT POOP

Deer scat looks different in the spring because deer eat more fresh green plants then.

DEER SCAT: SPRING / SUMMER

DEER SCAT: FALL / WINTER

RABBIT SCAT

JELLYBEANS

"This scat is from a deer, not a rabbit," said Mom.

"You can tell by the shape." added Dad. "Bunny poop is little brown balls. Deer scat is shaped more like jellybeans."

Michael found some marks in the dirt. "Are these deer tracks?" he asked.

"Yes!" said Mom. "They're from a mule deer. See how they're split? Deer hooves have two parts."

"What are these little marks?" asked Emily. She was starting to get interested.

"Those are from its dew claws," said Mom. "They're little claws behind the hoof. Dew claws sometimes show in deer tracks in soft ground. Lots of other animals have dew claws, too, including cats and dogs."

17

"Oh, no!" said Michael. Here's one
of its antlers. Did a bear eat the deer?"
Michael looked around nervously.

Dad bent down by the antler.
"This deer didn't get eaten. Its antler fell off.
Deer shed their antlers every winter
and then grow a new, bigger set
the next year."

the STRAIGHT
POOP

Female deer, elk, and moose
don't grow antlers. Reindeer
are the only members of the
deer family in which both males
and females have antlers.

"This deer was in a hurry, though," said Mom, as she studied the ground.

Michael and Emily went over to look.

"How can you tell?" said Emily. She was having fun finding all the clues the animals left behind.

19

"The hoofprints get very far apart here," Mom explained, "and the back prints are in front of the front prints."

"It was walking backwards?" said Emily.

"No, it was galloping. Something scared it and it was moving fast." Mom said.

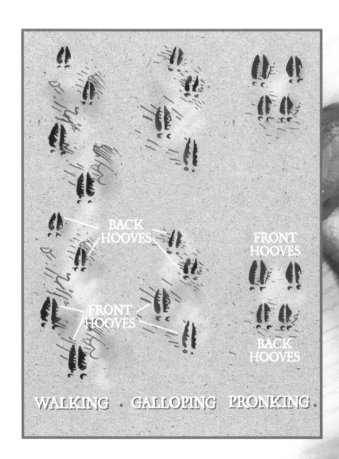

BACK HOOVES

FRONT HOOVES

FRONT HOOVES

BACK HOOVES

WALKING · GALLOPING PRONKING

GALLOP

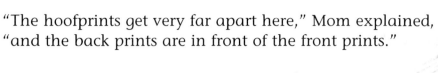

the STRAIGHT POOP

Sometimes mule deer bounce along with all four feet hitting the ground together. This is called "stotting" or "pronking."

the STRAIGHT
POOP

Y ou can tell what a skunk has been eating by looking at its scat. Things its body can't digest come out in the scat, such as feathers, mouse fur, and insects.

"Do you think that skunk scared the deer?" asked Michael.

Mom replied, "I don't think so, Michael. Skunks don't bother anyone if they're left alone."

"Then let's leave this one alone!" said Emily.

"Here's what scared the deer,"
Dad said. "There are coyote tracks
and scat all around here."

"Some of the tracks are small, like
they're from pups," said Mom.
"I'll bet their den is nearby."

the STRAIGHT POOP

Coyotes eat just about anything they can catch, and steal leftovers from other predators, too.

"They look like dog tracks," said Michael.

"That's because the coyote is a member of the dog family," explained Dad.

"Let's head back to camp for lunch, and then we can look for more tracks in Sequoia National Park this afternoon," said Mom.

the STRAIGHT POOP

One way to recognize coyote scat is by the hair and bits of bones in it. These are not found in dog scat.

By that afternoon, Michael was so excited about looking for more scat and tracks that he completely forgot about being scared of bears.

As they entered Sequoia National Park, Michael said, "Look, everyone! I found another coyote track."

24

"Let's see," said Dad. "This track doesn't show any claw marks, and the front of the big pad looks dented in. It looks more like a cat track than a dog track."

COYOTE TRACKS

BOBCAT TRACKS

MOUNTAIN LION TRACKS

"It's too big to be a bobcat track. I'll bet it's from a mountain lion," said Mom.

the STRAIGHT POOP

Cats can retract their claws, so their tracks don't show claw marks.

The only dog tracks that don't show claw marks are those of the gray fox. Its claws are so small and sharp that it can climb trees like a cat.

MOUNTAIN LION

BOBCAT

the STRAIGHT
POOP

Even though mountain lions are the biggest cats in America, they bury their scat just like housecats do.

You'll rarely see bobcat or mountain lion scat in the wild.

"Are they as big as panthers?" Michael asked, wide-eyed.

"Mountain Lions *are* panthers," Mom said. "Cougars, painters, pumas, and catamounts. They have lots of names!"

27

"Wow! There's a huge pile of scat right here in the middle of the trail," called Michael. "Is it from a mountain lion?"

Dad said, "Let's look closely. I can see grass and oats in the scat, so it couldn't be from a meat-eater like a mountain lion."

the STRAIGHT
POOP

Horses can poop while they walk, but they stop and stand still to pee.

"It's horse poop!" Emily guessed.

"Right," said Mom. "People ride horses out here. See if you can find any tracks."

Michael found tracks, all right, but they didn't look like he expected.
"This hoof print looks funny," he said.

Horses that are ridden a lot have metal shoes attached to their hooves to protect them from wear. Horse tracks show the shape of the shoe.

DEER TRACKS

HORSE TRACKS

HORSESHOE TRACKS

"Horses don't have split hooves like deer," said Dad. "Horse hooves have just one part."

"I think he's talking about the horseshoes," Mom said. "They make the hoof prints look different."

Michael looked up.
"What are these white
streaks on the rocks
over here?" he asked.

"That's called guano,"
said Dad.

the STRAIGHT POOP

Bats sleep hanging upside-down and like to perch in caves, trees, and holes in the rock.

"I know what that is!"
Emily. "We learned about
it in school. Guano is bat poop!"

"That's right," said Mom.
"There are a lot of different bats
in Sequoia and Kings Canyon
National Parks. Spotted
bats are really pretty and
have very big ears."

"Do they suck blood like vampires?" said Michael with a shudder.

"Oh no, they just eat bugs," Mom said with a smile. "There are no vampire bats around here."

the STRAIGHT POOP

Bat guano makes very good fertilizer. People buy bags of it to spread in their gardens to keep their plants healthy.

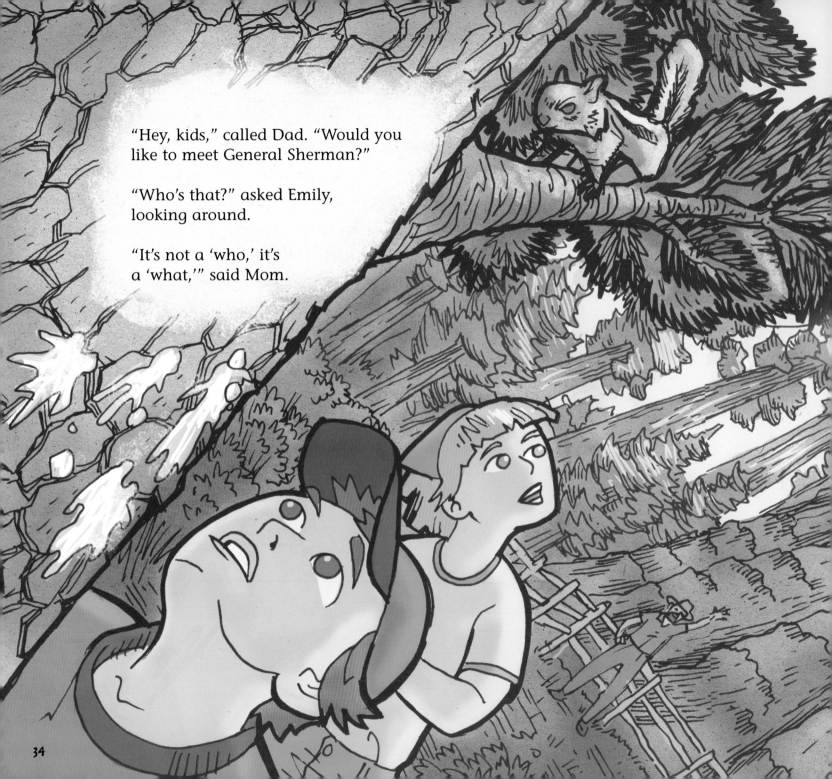

"Hey, kids," called Dad. "Would you like to meet General Sherman?"

"Who's that?" asked Emily, looking around.

"It's not a 'who,' it's a 'what,'" said Mom.

"The General Sherman tree is a sequoia," said Dad. "It's the biggest tree in the world."

"Sequoia trees can be hundreds of feet tall," Mom added.

the STRAIGHT POOP

The General Sherman tree weighs as much as ten blue whales, is almost as tall as the Statue of Liberty, and is probably more than 2,000 years old.

GENERAL SHERMAN
275 feet

STATUE OF LIBERTY
305 feet

Emily noticed something strange on the tree.

"Is this more bat poop?" she asked.

"That poop is from a great gray owl," Dad said. He looked down at the ground below the tree and added, "See these tracks with two toes pointing forward and two pointing back, and the owl pellets around the base of the tree?"

"Owl pellets?" said Emily.

"Owls eat their prey whole," explained Dad. "The parts they can't digest, like hair and bones, get coughed up in a pellet like this."

the STRAIGHT
POOP

Studying owl pellets is a great way to find out what owls eat. They dine on small animals such as mice, birds, and lizards.

"Yuck!" said the kids.

"You can tell this was
a big owl by the size
of the tracks and the
pellets," said Mom.
"The bigger the owl,
the bigger the owl pellets."

"There are a bunch
of different owls around Sequoia
and Kings Canyon National Parks,"
said Dad, "My favorite is the great gray owl."

the STRAIGHT
POOP

Owls see very well at night,
but they aren't blind during
the day, as some people believe.
They see just fine then, too.

38

"Whoa! Why is all of the bark torn off this tree?" Michael asked. "Did another porcupine do that?"

"This is different," replied Mom. "An animal was sharpening its claws on this tree, not eating the bark."

"And if you look how high those scratch marks go, it was pretty big!" added Mom.

"It's not just the animal that's big," said Emily. "Look at the size of this poop!"

"It looks like we found your black bear," said Mom. "Let's see what you learned today. What can you figure out about this bear?"

"It's been eating plants," said Emily, "because there's no hair or bones in this poop."

"Good job!" Mom said. "What else?"

the STRAIGHT POOP

Black bears eat almost anything. They mostly dine on leaves, nuts, berries, insects, twigs, and honey, but they also hunt small animals and fish.

"It must be as tall as you, and it has really long claws," said Michael.

"Here's the bear's footprint," said Michael. "It's really big, and it has more toes than a coyote or mountain lion."

"I told you you'd be able to count a black bear's toes," laughed Mom.

"It rubbed off some hair on the tree," said Emily. "You said this was a black bear, but these hairs are reddish brown."

"Black bears can be all different colors," explained Mom. "They can be black, brown, or cinnamon-colored, like this one. There are even black bears that are almost white."

As the family ate dinner that night, everyone talked about how much fun they had.

"We didn't see very many animals," said Emily, "but it seemed like we did."

Everyone laughed when Michael said, "And I didn't get scared once!"

45

TRACKS and

ANIMALS THAT EAT BOTH PLANTS AND OTHER ANIMALS:

ANIMALS THAT EAT ONLY PLANTS:

BLACK BEAR

Large tracks with five visible toes and claws.

Scat changes depending on diet but usually contains vegetation.

BRUSH RABBIT

Small tracks are filled in between the toes.

The scat is in little brown balls.

PORCUPINE

Front track shows four toes, back track shows five. Tail drag marks are usually visible.

Scat pellets are larger than deer scat.

MULE DEER

Pointy split-hoof tracks.

Scat is long and oval-shaped like jellybeans, not round like a rabbit's.

HORSE

Tracks are much bigger than deer tracks, and not split.

Scat is in chunks, with roughage from vegetation often visible.

SCAT NOTES

ANIMALS THAT EAT ONLY OTHER ANIMALS:

COYOTE

Tracks are like a dog's, with four toes, usually with visible claw marks.

Scat is very dark colored with tapered ends and usually contains hair.

MOUNTAIN LION

Tracks are bigger than a coyote's, but claws don't show.

Scat is rarely seen because they bury it.

BOBCAT

Tracks are very similar to a mountain lion's, but about half the size.

Scat is usually buried.

SPOTTED BAT

Bats rarely land on soft ground to leave tracks.

Scat is runny and white.

GREAT GRAY OWL

Tracks show four toes: two pointing forward and two back or sideways.

Scat is runny and white. "Cough pellets" contain fur and bones.

ABOUT the AUTHOR and ILLUSTRATOR

GARY ROBSON lives on a ranch near Yellowstone National Park in Montana and owns a bookstore in Red Lodge. He received his teaching credential in 1987 and has taught in California and Montana colleges. He is an expert in closed captioning technology for deaf and hard-of-hearing people. In addition to the *Who Pooped?* series, Gary has written five other nonfiction books. www.whopooped.com

ROBERT RATH is a book designer and illustrator living in Bozeman, Montana. Although he has worked with Scholastic Books, Lucasfilm, and Montana State University, his favorite project is keeping up with his family.

Who Pooped? in the Park?™

OTHER BOOKS IN THE WHO POOPED IN THE PARK?™ SERIES:

Acadia National Park

Glacier National Park

Grand Canyon National Park

Grand Teton National Park

Great Smoky Mountains National Park

Olympic National Park

Red Rock Canyon National Conservation Area

Rocky Mountain National Park

Shenandoah National Park

Sonoran Desert

Yellowstone National Park

Yosemite National Park